Giorgio Rosa

Rose Island

The real story of an utopian micronation

Paolo Emilio Persiani

piazza San Martino 9/C
40126 Bologna

Tel. (+39) 051/9913920
Fax (+39) 051/19901229

e–mail: info@persianieditore.com
www.persianieditore.com

Edited by Giorgia Dolci, Maria Vella

Editorial staff: Carlo D'Alonzo, Loris Di Bella

The Publisher is at persons entitled's disposal
for unidentified iconographic sources

INDEX

PUBLISHER'S PREFACE

Goodbye Giorgio. Heartful thanks

I will be mourning the loss of Dr Giorgio Rosa, a dear friend of mine and author of our publishing company. When I first met him, a ground-breaking, adventurous world has opened up to me. This world had been created in 1968 and was full of challenges that took place in our delightful Romagna seas. It was amazing, I always heard of it, but never experienced myself. This man before me was the first one to have made a romantic, anarchical and revolutionary dream come true. A dream that I, ideally, followed too.

This vision was also shared with other free men and not just with great anarchists, such as Michail Bakunin, Errico Malatesta and Curzio Malaparte, but also with ordinary men, who did not want to depend on any political organization. If the lowest common denominator of anarchist currents had been the necessity to cancel the State or every kind of established power, Dr Rosa had paradoxically managed to do it through the constitution of this new nation of his own invention. Thus, this has to be the reading key of Rose Island story.

It was in the year 2008, that Dr Rosa thoroughly kept telling me his stories which seemed to have happened just the day before. Forty years had passed but his eyes were shining and still reflected his deep faith in what he had done. Unfortunately, David was defeated by Goliath, as we all know. His friendship has honoured me for all these years. Our conversations covered the widest range of topics, from trips to Rosa's studies about constructing materials (that still remain one of the Island's secret), through military history, a great passion of his.

One day, as I was visiting his studio situated near Giardini Margherita[1] something came to my mind. Why not start collecting any tiny detail of this outstanding adventure so that I could have later published a filmed interview? I did not want all this preciousness to fade with time and, most importantly, I wanted the entire world to know the injustice occurred in our seas. So, I plunged myself into work. I tried to enrich my material as much as I could, putting every kind of illustration and contribution of Dr Rosa's archive together. From that moment on, the public's interest kindled, finally awakening from a general indifference that helped the government sink the whole story. Despite his age, Rosa came to present the documentary himself, along with his entire family. As his publisher, I am doubly grateful for this. Afterwards, several DVDs and books have been issued. I would like to remember one in particular: Walter Veltroni's book, in which I have been mentioned more than once; therefore, I would like to thank him publicly.

Lastly, a big special thanks goes to Dr Rosa and his son Lorenzo for their constant kindness, fondness, and goodwill towards me. Am I to grow old too, I will have the privilege to tell my sons and grandchildren about this extraordinary person I met and who I shall meet again.

Paolo Emilio Persiani

---

1 One of the biggest parks in Bologna *[Ed]*.

Giorgio Rosa's memorial
Between thunderbolt and storm

ROSE ISLAND'S THUNDERBOLT AND STORM

What was Rose Island for me?

Everything, I can tell you that!

It was 1956, my new home in Pilastro[1] was almost done and thanks to my steady contact with papers and offices, I became aware of how the United States had enslaved our population.

Politicians did not want us to do anything and everything was becoming every day more and more oppressing. Priests thought about spreading their absurdities and sects they were parts of and did not have ears for other opinions. Communists tried to boycott other men's lots of lands and existence. Only politicians had a future, doesn't matter if they were supported by Russians or Americans. At that point, I even considered to leave my country to reach an independent one, where smart people were in charge and idiots obeyed. I am and always have been a free man. Yet two reasons took a stand against my thought: firstly, religion and sects are, by now, rooted

---

1 Bologna's neighbourhood *[Ed]*.

in every culture; secondly, I would have felt guilty to walk away from my nation, from my city and my family, a core for my survival.

Then, when the idea of building my own freedom first made way in my mind. Bright people would have led the way, while feckless people would have gotten kicked out.

Everything needed to be created from scratch. But needs are the basis for modern civilization. My research began: I read about British Isles outside territorial waters, I talked to prosecutors, and Dr Sereni in particular, one of the greatest teachers in our University. Finally, my idea was taking shape, legally speaking. As regards construction, I was pretty sure I had all necessary knowledge to build what I needed. The day after, the patent number 1799/A/68 was born. Now the tough part came. I had to take a very long time away from teaching and my professional engineering career but, eventually, I came up with a plan. On the mainland I would have built a sort of steel pipes frame, then closed their nozzles and brought them till the selected spot floating (outside Italian territorial waters, of course). What was the perfect spot, you may ask? In the open waters near Rimini, a popular city along Riviera, whose highway was then being built.

All the set up was hard and expensive. Firstly, I needed a full nautical education, and this led me to a scrupulous inspection on my future Eden's spot. I figured out which equipment or connections could better work for me and which law allowed me to do all of this. It turned out that from two leagues (about 11.112 meters) outside Italian coasts, I could do whatever I wanted. Everyone agreed on this.

Therefore, I was once and for all convinced. Only later I have been told that I should have made agreements with Masonry or Mafia and maybe this was my mistake. I always leaned on trusted friends and for two years I had been visiting the oil platform – such as Sarom in Ravenna – and studying how to place all the pipes offshore. I considered to accumulate sand through dredges, while the atmosphere in Italy became increasingly tyrannical and, as engineer freelance and professor, I realized it every day more and more. In the meantime, I was working on determining where exactly 11.500 m from the Italian coast were.

Never have I ever recruited an equipment. My journeys at sea were possible thanks to a steel motor board, handmade by me, using a Fiat 500 engine that never betrayed me. During the summer of 1960, I went to Rimini twice a week, where I rented a shed in order to conduct my searches. I travelled by land thanks to my 1100 Fiat car. It took me just one hour to drive from via Frino to Rimini pier. Meanwhile, I also prepared some luminous lights (i.e. buoys, etc.) that would have been essential to make my Island visible. I tested on the selected point and indicated as "Z", figuring out the water draft was about 13,40 m at high tide. Throughout the year 1960 I have been studying and keeping in touch with Rimini, helped by Lella, my wife, by people from Rimini (including Mr Rinaldini, the owner of a shipyard) and many others. In Chioggia I bought a *mototopo*[2] that would have been useful for safer waterborne transport.

However, due to occupational commitment I decided to drop this idea. It was 1962 and I had rather kept up with my research in Bologna.

---

2 Typical vessel of the venetian tradition *[Ed]*.

Two years had passed before I found energy and courage back.

As a matter of fact, on 30th May 1964 I started a new trip in order to catch up with my old friends and spread some positivity throughout the team, which would have helped brighten up the work environment. I called Rimini Port Authority, as long as Ravenna's and Pesaro's to agree on dock grants and refuelling (that was tax-free considering the unusual position, that's why it needed a special treatment).

So I called Dalmine Company, one of the biggest pipes producers in Italy and I ordered every piece necessary. I got them delivered to Pesaro, where they could have directly been assembled and welded, while I had to buy a fishing boat – Bruno I – that added up to my dear Luciano (the venetian *mototopo*) and my homemade motor board that just later was delivered from Bologna to Rimini by train.

In July, my Dalmine pipes reached Pesaro and, on the 14th, the whole structure was finished and ready to be launched. As I said, the procedure was easy: each of the nine pipes was closed both on top and at the bottom. Here, they had a slider that would have opened just when the pipes were floating on the sea. This way, they would have taken on water, going upright to the sea bottom. No scuba diver was needed, so that everyone could work perfectly safe.

The launching itself was, however, no easy job. We had to use two tugboats in order to drag everything to the right spot. The job was finished on the 31ˢᵗ July morning. Next steps that I needed to deal with: hiring some workmen to secure beams on top of the pipes and waiting for Dr Vicinelli, the surveyor in charge of nailing everything on the sea bottom. He did not show up until 28ᵗʰ August. On 29ᵗʰ he had an on-site inspection, but the measurements were not taken correctly and only on 9ᵗʰ September we figured out that the missing piece was two meters shorter than it should have been. Edipali Company sent us another one, that was assembled on 21ˢᵗ September. Building works were proceeding too slowly, and winter was coming. In fact, on 13ᵗʰ February 1965 the whole framework was overturned. Thanks to Società Adriatica's help (a company from Ancona), we managed to put everything back in order in May of the same year. The fixing operation, costs aside, was extremely successful and I could soon proceed to stipulate a new contract with Ferrari Company, in Casalecchio di Reno (BO), who helped me with the last fastening operations.

On 8th September 1965 Rimini Port Authority wanted to withdraw my permission to use their dock, with no reason. I opposed myself firmly and they eventually accepted their defeat, even though they kept being informed about my progresses. Things were tough, either for the necessity to find suitable workers or for the sea storm that slowed down our works. On 21st May 1966 I was the first man on earth to sleep on my Island and even today I still feel excited and emotional just thinking of all I have been through.

Among the dates I better recall there is the 6th November, when "Sorrisi e Canzoni" magazine published an article about my Island. On 23rd November 1966 Mr Sanguinetti, Rimini Port Authority's colonel, gave me an ultimatum: whether I shut down everything, or I had to ask Eni[3] for an authorization (but I have been wondering: why should I have asked for a permission for an area that does not belong to any Italian company?).

---

3 Which stands for *Ente Nazionale Idrocarburi*, Italy's National Hydrocarbon Corporation *[Ed]*.

Later on, on 23rd January 1967, Rimini police chief Mr Pagliarulo asked me if everything I had been doing was experimental, and it actually was. On 8th February I talked about customs and material export to Dr Martelli; on 5th November I assured him that the island was built 6,5 miles away from the Italian court. On 3rd March I had a meeting with Dr Zullino, director of "Epoca" magazine, to talk about my experience.

Also "Novella 2000" contacted me and, in May 1967, I found at 280 m depth freshwater. Again, in June 1967 colonel Sanguinetti threatened me saying that I definitely needed Rimini dock's agreement to restock. This is why on 10th June I presented him an informational report about what was going on, on my Island.

On 20th August 1967, friends and acquaintances begged me to let them visit my new Eden. It was officially viable. The walkable floor area was about 400 m², but the project was to build a five-floor building above it. For the moment, just the first two were made. I studied a way to enclose the vessels landing area, which I later did, using some filled-up-with-freshwater rubber tube, so that they would weigh less than sea water and, therefore, float.

However, on 25th June 1968 the Italian police, Carabinieri[4] and Guardia di Finanza[5] surrounded Rose Island with roughly ten pilot boats and occupied it

---

4 National military police of Italy, policing both military and civilian populations *[Ed]*.

5 Finance Guard, the authority of the Ministry of Finance and part of the Italian armed forces *[Ed]*.

militarily. This action definitely violated international laws but, apparently, the U. S. and their servant, Italy, are used to it.

I should point out that on the island there was no gun, no wanted person, no drugs or anything against Italy or its laws. And so we witnessed to the Italian military occupation of the Free Rose Island that already possessed a Constitution and a Government composed of people from Bologna who yearned for freedom too.

A great *tour de force* between me and Italy began. All hell broke loose when they would not let me dock on my own Island (me, the owner!) and kept Mr Piero Ciavatta (the guardian of the island) and his wife captives. I immediately sent a telegram to Saragot, then the president of the Italian Republic, who did not even answer me. Now, two years later, I am pretty sure that it was my conversation with Barnabà del Sid to get the ball rolling.

I must also say that father Albino Ciccanti (one of the major experts of Esperanto language) helped me out translating everything, since Esperanto was our official language.

During the first days of July lots of requests to purchase my Island arrived and, on the 11th, Piero was released and came to me straight away.

Monteceneri Radio also took our matter at heart, helped by Dr Umberto Lazzari. Other people, such as avv.[6] Grassani and avv. Marchesini, both from Bologna. On the 7th August I was interrogated by the

6 Abbreviation for *avvocato*, Italian for *lawyer*. Since there is no universally accepted translation (J.D. is used just in academic context, Esq. is often felt as too pretentious), I decided to keep the Italian one, to avoid any misunderstandings *[Ed]*.

police and I found out that they had been tapping all our calls (long live freedom!).

On 28th August I drove to Rome and handed out my written protest (of which I already served notice to the Rimini Port Authority on the day before) to the Council of State Office and I learned that my court hearing had been scheduled for 27th September. My document was approved by Dr Letizia and Dr Ceccherini. On 4th September Dr Lazzari had a talk with Council of State's supervisor who ensured a successful ending.

About 20 days later the names of the 6th section of State Council were released: Vincenzo Uccellatore, Carlo Anelli, Mario Gora, Lorenzo Quonzo, Mario Egidio Schinoia, Alfano Quaranta; its secretary was Dr Pasquale Del Po, phone number 06-65.26.93, NUI 22. File's number was 756/68.

On 30th September a demolition estimated for about 30 million Lira[7] has been done, but later on it was found out that the Italian Government did not have the money! For the time being, every transaction was suspended. A Government Officer explicitly said that

---

7 About 15.500 euro *[Ed]*.

if the U. S. gave them the approval for a demolition, I would have been doomed.

On 6th October 1968 avv. Praga proposed an appeal to his Excellency Catalano in Strasbourg. I even got word that both judges Cuonzo and Gaia stand on our side, but the others clearly received orders from above.

On 15th October 1968 brigadier Biscardi and Dr Olivieri from Bologna informed us that there was a great deal of magazines from Copenhagen addressed to Insula de la Rosoi, which helped us safeguard our freedom. On the first November 1968 I had a talk to senator Bersani, who was sick; even avv. Cucci showed interest.

On November 18th both Catalano and Cucci asked for an expert witness report. Their intention was to stretch things out, considering that Italian Government already agreed to 31 million euros costs to demolish my platform.

Some days later, avv. Catalano expressed his suspicion about we being "manipulated" by an outside power. Three days after, every removable thing was taken away from the island and brought to the mainland. Italian Navy was ready to blow it up. Avv. Praga phoned Catalano to personally deliver him the good news. At that point I talked to Mr Gorini, who helped me request a written explanation on the Government's behaviour. Both Nenni, Preti, Mancini, Brodolini and Tanassi got a telegram about it.

On 3rd December, there was the oath for the preventive technical assessment of Dr Giuseppe Lombi with an office in via Principe Amedeo in Rimini. He needed five months to carry out the assignment. Port Authority scheduled their inspection on 10th December 1968 that later, unfortunately, had been cancelled due to a sea storm.

A friend of mine, Berti, had a meeting with congressman Preti, who did not want to hear a single word about the matter. Avv. Gozzi and avv. Roma gathered to discuss my situation on 17th September. Soon after, the Government was said to care just for pride. It was all about their principles. The Military Order of Malta's opinion was that everything was too compromised by that moment. Yet, on 21st December, Rimini's magistrate urged the commissioned people to do the inspection as soon as possible.

So they did: on 23ʳᵈ December my Island was being inspected; then the inventory of what had been taken away was written down (just later I noticed that many of my things were stolen, like my foghorn, some gears, etc…). Some suggested to donate everything to the Esperantists.

On 28ᵗʰ December evening I was at Villa Verrucchio with Mr Dosi to finally meet up with Hon. Preti, who made his lack of interest in my cause very clear. About one month later Rose Island was about to get destroyed.

I have been interviewed by Prof Montemaggi, to whom I said that I was «ashamed to be Italian», but my statement was never mentioned in his article.

On 11th February 1969 Rose Island was undermined with 75 kg dynamite on each pipe. Yet the structure did not succumb. Some days after they tried again, this time with 120 kg dynamite per pipe: it warped, but did not surrender. Only squalls and sea storms definitely wiped it out on 26 February 1969. It was

officially communicated by "Gazzettino Emilia-Romagna" on the same day.

Still, I did not give up. Once again, I contacted the Sovereign Military Order of Malta that, frankly, found my situation so degenerated that they thought intervening would have been useless. Many papers claimed the demolition to be null and void, since Italy had no rights on that spot.

As the result of my petition, the European Parliament simply answered me that the Island was outside European laws, therefore they could not have a say in this. Italy never returned the piled-up I.G.E.[8] and other prestigious people (Nicola Catalano from Rome and Gianfranco Gagliani from Rimini) showed their interest in the matter.

Even the Port Authority of Rimini charged 436.000 lire of interests on the sums advanced for the demolition of the island (see communication of frigate captain Carlo Nardi of 25th October 1974 with practice n. 11298334).

---

8 A turnover tax *[Ed]*.

To better understand this whole situation, I had better attach a historical documentation such as:

1. My patent, released only after Italy's conquest;
2. Act of Incorporation of the Free Territory;
3. Offices' division and a copy of G. Lombi's written report, attachments included;
4. Facsimile posters against Italy's demolition of Rose Island that papered the city of Rimini.

I must ultimately add that I still have been in contact with Mr Vacchelli, Marzulo, Versace and Dalmine. Not to mention the amount of people – as Prezzolini from Lugano on the 28th July – that wrote about Rimini nightclubs.

I usually like to recall that for a short period of time my Island had a post office, where I even issued stamps; I chose an orange triangle with three red roses in the middle of it as our national flag.

I would also like to remember all the people that supported me throughout this long journey, as Mr

Ghellaus from Bonn, Dr Fabio Fiore who wrote a novel about my Island, avv. Gagliani who handed me the extract of the international organization code, Mr Dasi, Dr Philippe Chaier (15 Avenue Eugene Pittard in Geneve), Mr Richard King (20 Wetherby Gdns, London SW5), legal advisor Gottfried Dubach from San Vittore di Mesolcina in Switzerland, European Parliament's esperantist Stanislao Boscarino (via Vittorio Veneto 92, Ragusa), Malta opposition party's President Prof. Worbek, Dr A. Buttigreg (Laour Party Hamrum, Malta).

So why was Italy so ruthless against Rose Island? Maybe Eni's interests were the key. They feared that we would have drilled gas and then sell it. But to whom? And "Resto del Carlino" lack of support was because maybe they had some arrangements with Eni as well. This is proved by Hon. Preti's indifference, he was even called for support twice, but both times refused it.

Later I got asked to build another island near Algeria to have some springboards, or even to put up a hotel at sea (this last suggestion was made by Piera Montanari, viale Carducci 13, Bologna). And again: proposals by Mr Bates from Principality of Sealand, by avv. Mister Arthur A. Stefan (Suite 717, Ring Building, Washington D.C.) and King Oliver (130 Ashley Gardens SW1P 1HL, England).

I will attach three more documents below:

1. Preventive Technical Investigation, made by Giuseppe Lombi;
2. Stamp Issues before and after Italy's destruction;
3. Island's official flag.

In conclusion, I will just say that freedom is a pipe dream and whoever holds power wants to keep it at all costs. Minister of Interior's relentlessness remains to me inexplicable, but he died before he could be embroiled in Mani Pulite (Italian for "clean hands"), a juridical investigation that involved Democrazia Cristiana party.

I also believe that Demo Christian Government's hostility was all about their worry that I would have built a casino. And this would have meant a terrible risk for them: therefore, they decided to strongly oppose, forgetting about international laws too.

Giorgio Rosa

Photographic book

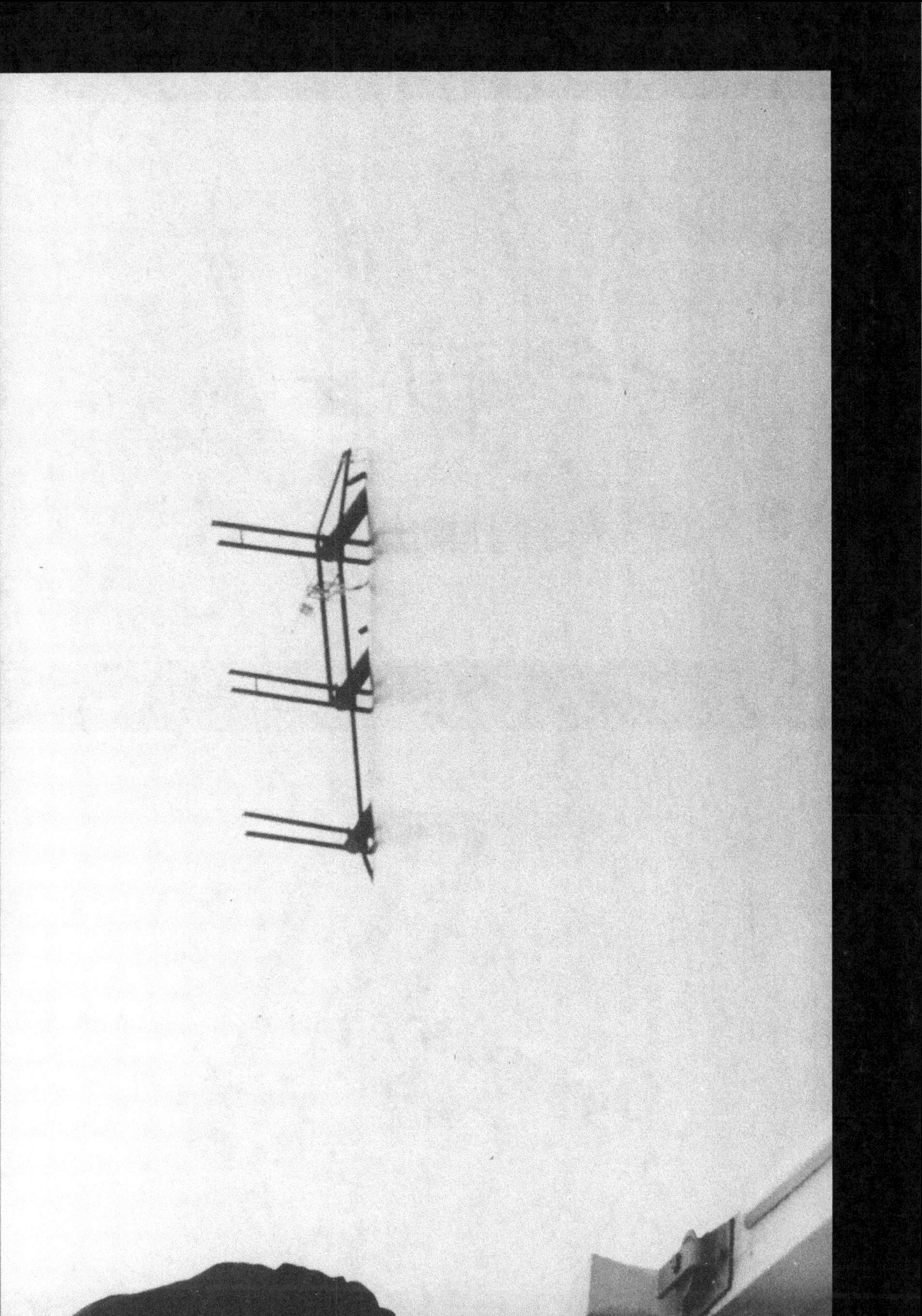

THILCO

FAEMA
E 61

THILCO
FAEMA
E 61

T/2

T/2

Philately

L.T. INSULO DE LA ROZOJ

L.T. INSULO   DE LA ROZOJ

This volume was printed
on December 2020 on behalf of

Casa Editrice Persiani